written and illustrated by
WARREN HANSON

TRISTAN PUBLISHING
Minneapolis

Library of Congress Cataloging-in-Publication Data

Hanson, Warren.
  Today's special / written and illustrated by Warren Hanson.
     p. cm.
  ISBN 978-0-931674-82-2 (hardcover : alk. paper)
  I. Title.
  PS3558.A54378T63 2010
  813'.54--dc22

                                    2010008846

TRISTAN PUBLISHING, INC.
2355 Louisiana Avenue North
Golden Valley, MN 55427

Please visit us at:
www.tristanpublishing.com
books with a message

Contents

Thank you, Rebecca Joy.

TODAY'S SPECIAL

It's been a hard week. And it's only Wednesday. Things haven't been going well at work, so I need to do some traveling to see what I can do about it. That hasn't gone over very well at home, so there had been an argument on Monday morning as I was leaving. Nothing huge. But it's been on my mind.

My travels have taken me off the big highways and onto the two-lane roads that go through one small town after another, slowing me down and making me even more frustrated. I feel like I'm not getting anywhere.

It's almost noon, and the continental breakfast at last night's motel didn't amount to much. So in the next little town I come to, I look for a place to get something to eat. There are none of the usual fast food places or chain restaurants in a town this size, so I'm just going to have to take my chances.

The highway takes me right down Main Street. Angle parking. Pickup trucks. I see several of them parked in front of a place called "Irene's Cafe," a typical small town hash house. It doesn't look very promising, but it's probably the only place in town. I park between a pickup and a Buick and walk in.

The door jingles cheerfully as I enter. The air inside is slightly steamy and filled with the smells of comfort food. Gravy and grease, fresh-baked buns and coffee. All those homey smells are stirred together by the slow-spinning ceiling fan in the middle of the room.

The place is pretty clean, considering how old it must be. The walls are an almost-bright yellow, probably painted that color over thirty years ago. Repainting now would be a huge job, with so many trinkets and bowling trophies, framed letters and faded photographs crowding those walls, along with Irene's collection of plates from around the world.

Three booths line one wall, with two along the other, allowing room for a couple of extra chairs, a stack of kids' booster seats, and a high chair with a bright yellow plastic tray. There are some tables, and a counter at the back with a few stools. Behind that is a long rectangular window into the kitchen, with several small green pieces of paper with orders written on them hanging from the top. I can see a guy with dark hair and a baseball cap, squinting through the smoke that rises from the grill.

There are quite a few customers here, a good sign, and the murmur of their voices mixes with the smells in the air to give Irene's Cafe a comfortable, welcoming feel.

I sit down at an empty booth next to the front window. The dark red seat covering is ancient and cracked, and a single menu in a clear plastic sleeve stands on the table, held up between the sugar jar and the napkin dispenser, while the ketchup, salt and pepper loiter nearby. The waitress is there immediately with a warm smile and a glass of water. Her plastic name tag says "Irene."

"Be with ya in a minute. Coffee?"

I say yes and she heads back to the kitchen, smoothly checking every table in the place to make sure that everyone is taken care of. I'm about to pick up the menu when I notice a framed chalkboard hanging on the wall, between the coat rack by the front door and the revolving glass pie case. Across the top of the chalkboard, in colorful silk-screened letters, it says "Today's Special." And below that, in the area where I would expect to see the featured menu items of the day, someone has chalked only this: "Yes it is."

GRATITUDE

Sitting in a booth by herself with her back toward the front window is a woman who looks to be in her mid-seventies. She is dressed better than you'd expect someone having lunch at Irene's to be dressed. Not rich or fancy. But dignified and respectful, like for church.

The table in front of her is covered with papers, photographs, letters and scrapbooks. There is only room left for one pretty teacup, which is pushed way over against the wall, to avoid an unfortunate spill.

Her movements are slow. Not because of age, but because of reverence. She touches each photo, affectionately picks up each letter, lovingly turns the pages of the albums, savoring the memories that are spread out before her.

"More tea, Ellen?" says Irene, approaching the table quietly, speaking in a half whisper, not wanting to disturb the woman's thoughts. Not many people order tea here, but Irene keeps it on hand for Ellen.

"Oh, yes. Thank you, Irene. I got a little chilly out at the cemetery. I took flowers." She picks up a photo from the table as Irene holds the cup and pours, careful to hold it well away from the table. The black and white photo is of a young bride and groom. "It would have been fifty years today."

"I'll bet you miss him." Irene cautiously puts the full cup back in its safe place near the wall.

"Yes. Yes, I miss him every day. Sometimes I have a hard time believing he's gone." She passes her open hand over everything spread before her on the table. "But look at all he gave me, Irene. Just look at all we had together."

Even though the cafe is busy with the lunch rush, Irene stands patiently, with a pot of hot tea water in her hand and a look of genuine kindness on her face, as Ellen picks up item after item from her collection of memories and talks about each one.

"This is from our trip to Quebec for our first anniversary. Chet didn't tell me where we were going. We stopped at Niagara Falls and he bought me this bracelet in a little gift shop. I thought we were going to stay there, but he said there was something even better ahead. We stayed at the Frontenac. Here's a picture. It was so beautiful. He said he wanted me to feel like a queen. Oh, and I did!

"Here's Chet with the twins, trying to keep them both swinging at the same time. He was such a good dad. So patient. And he loved to teach them things. About the world. Later they would joke that whenever they asked him a question, he would always start his answer with the beginning of the universe. He said he wanted them to understand the big picture." She smiles.

Ellen shows Irene several other bits of memorabilia — newspaper clippings, foreign stamps, tickets from plays and cruises and national parks — and talks about each item and each memory with genuine joy and appreciation. Then a noise from one of the other tables makes her realize that she is keeping Irene from her work.

She looks up from her tableful of memories. "Today's special, Irene. I don't want to waste it being sad. I want to spend this day being grateful for what we had together. For all those years we shared, and all these wonderful memories we created. I want to remind myself of the beautiful life we had, and all the joy that life gave us. That's worth celebrating, don't you think?"

"It is. It sure is," says Irene as she starts to drift away.

"Tonight the kids and grandkids are coming, and we're going to celebrate this 50th wedding anniversary. I even bought champagne!"

Gratitude. It means being glad for all that we have been given. Knowing that our cup is always more full than empty. Today is a good day for appreciating what we have, rather than regretting what we don't.

BELIEVING

"Look, Grandpa. That lady has an angel."

A man in his late sixties and his three-year-old granddaughter are sitting in a booth next to the glass pie case. She is perched on a dark green booster seat and is looking at a patch of light dancing on the wall above a woman sitting by herself across the room.

The man looks over at the patch of light shimmering on the wall, then starts to look around for where it might be coming from. His granddaughter goes back to coloring on the back of the paper placemat with the crayons Irene has brought to the table in a fruit jar. The man soon sees a glass of water sitting on the table in the booth near the window. The opening and closing of the jingling cafe door, Irene's footsteps on the old wooden floor, and the moving air that's pushed around the room by the slow ceiling fan all work together to make the water in the glass shimmy in the sunlight that's pouring through the window.

"That's not an angel, Honey. It's light that's come all the way from the sun, way out in space. That light traveled millions and millions of miles just so it could come shining through that big front window. Now, see that glass of water on that table over there?"

He points, and the little girl lifts her head and looks toward the glass of water with indifference, then goes back to her coloring.

"That sunlight is bouncing off the top of the water in that glass, just like a rubber ball. And it bounces," he draws a trajectory through the air with his finger, "all the way across the room and lands on that wall above that lady's head. It's wiggling like that because the water in that glass is wiggling." He crosses his arms on the tabletop and leans forward toward his little granddaughter. "Understand?"

He's proud of himself for giving her this small science lesson.

The little girl answers without looking up. "I understand, Grandpa. I can see the angel, and you can't."

When does that happen? When do we start thinking that it's better to try to explain miracles than to just accept them? He sits there, silenced by a little girl's vision. Her faith. Her belief in everyday magic.

He remembers when he could see like that. When clouds were castles or flying horses instead of collections of water molecules clinging to specks of dust in the upper atmosphere. He remembers when the tooth fairy and magic beans and monsters under the bed were all very real. Before he grew up and knew so much. Before common sense stepped in to replace a sense of wonder.

He looks across the table at the swirls and scribbles of crayon that his granddaughter is making on the back of the placemat. "That's a nice picture, Honey. What is it?"

"Grandpa! Can't you see?" She holds the picture up. "It's your house. See? There's your big chair. And that's you and me. And there's your 'frigerator. And Grandma is driving her car. And there's a dog who wants to live with you. See? Right there."

He looks at her scribbles. "Oh, yes, yes. Now I see it! I was looking at it upside down before.

Does the dog have a name?"

"Peaches!" She says it with the joy of discovery, like she just learned it herself.

He smiles, thinks for a minute, then asks, "Would it be okay if I drew a picture, too?"

She shrugs. "Okay."

"Can I use one of these crayons?"

"Sure, Grandpa. They're for everybody. But don't use the purple one, 'cause that's just for on Sunday."

He turns over his placemat and takes a blue crayon out of the jar. He thinks briefly about trying to draw something real, like an airplane or a fish. Then he stops to realize that, although he often tries to teach her things about the world, about the sun and water and reflections, here is a moment when she can teach him something. She can teach him to see again, like he once did when he was her age. She can give him, if even for just these few minutes, that sense of wonder and imagination that we seem to lose as we get older. So, instead of struggling to draw something real, he simply makes a few random scribbles on the paper. Then he proudly holds it up for her to see.

"Do you see what it is?"

She looks up from her own work, then tips her

head to one side and wrinkles her nose. "Grandpa! You know I can't read."

He looks at his chicken scratches, puzzled. Well, yes, it does kind of look like writing, though it doesn't actually say anything.

"Oh, I'll bet you can. Go ahead. What do you think it says?"

She wrinkles her nose again, then raises her shoulders and her eyebrows. "I love you?"

Just then Irene stops by the table with a glass of apple juice and a coffee pot. "How are we doin' over here? Are we having a good day?"

"We're having a great day, Irene. Today I saw

my very first angel. See there?"

He points to the shimmering light on the wall, and Irene turns to look.

"Well, what d'ya know! There is an angel over there!" Then she turns back and looks at the man with a knowing smile. "But, Charlie, you need to come in here more often. I see angels in this place every day."

Believing. It's easy to stop when we think we know all the answers. But this is a good day to look around for miracles and start believing again.

FORGIVENESS

Sitting at the counter near the back of the cafe are a middle-aged man and his teenage son. They are seated side by side, but facing the kitchen, not each other. The father has chosen the middle two of the four stools, hoping to discourage anyone else from sitting at the counter. In this busy and popular place, he is hoping for privacy.

"Why'd you wanna come here?" asks the sullen son. "This place is old and weird."

"I know it's not your kind of place anymore. But we used to come here a lot when you were little. You used to sit in that high chair right over there."

The teenager rolls his eyes but doesn't look toward the high chair.

"Besides, I figured that, in a busy place like this, we could talk without anybody listenin' in. And maybe without shoutin' at each other. We've had enough of that at home."

The boy lowers his head and hunches his shoulders. "So, what's this 'somethin' important' you hafta say?"

Irene steps in front of them and asks if they're ready to order. The teen asks for a cheeseburger, medium rare, with onion rings and a

Coke. His dad says, "Same for me," and the kid rolls his eyes again and flips his fork impatiently.

"Well,... there's actually two things. Jake, you know that what you did's been really hard for me and your mom. Really hard."

"I know, I know." He flips the fork irritably.

"We just couldn't imagine, when you were sittin' in that high chair over there, that you would grow up to do somethin' like this."

"Oh, man. Come on, Dad."

"Maybe that's too sentimental for you. But it's true. No parent expects their sweet little boy

— and you really were a sweet boy, Jake — no parent expects their kid to get in trouble with the law."

Jake, annoyed, says nothing, but lowers his head and hunches his shoulders one more notch, tapping the fork on the glass of Coke that Irene has just set down. Irene, uncharacteristically, walks away without a word.

"I don't wanna go through it all again. Why you did it. What you were thinkin'. Why you thought you wouldn't get caught. We've been through all that." The dad, still facing the kitchen, unable to look at his son, seems to be talking to himself. Irene brings the two cheeseburgers, and the dad reaches for the ketchup.

"There's been way too much anger spent on this." He lifts the top of the bun and douses his cheeseburger with ketchup, then passes the bottle to his son. "It hasn't got us anywhere."

Jake remains silent. He refuses to make eye contact with his dad and instead stares ahead, at the wall beneath the window into the kitchen. He eats one of the crisp, greasy onion rings, then licks his fingers as though he's not even listening.

"I still don't know any answers, Jake." The dad sets his cheeseburger down on the plate with both hands. "But I do know this." He pauses, as if he is bringing some kind of courage up from way down deep inside. He takes a slow breath. "I know that... I can't do this anymore. I can't live this way anymore. With the anger an' disappointment an' shame you brought to me and to your mother and to this family. I... I just can't."

Jake is listening now, and he feels his rage starting to boil inside. He knows that his dad is leading up to some big pronouncement, some ultimatum. Something the boy doesn't want to hear. His dad is about to swing a big, parental hammer, and Jake prepares himself to swing right back. He doesn't care who's in the cafe to see it.

"Jake, I don't know what that judge is gonna say this afternoon. I don't know what kind of punishment you're gonna get. That's all out of my hands. But I do know what I have to do."

He swivels on his stool and faces his son.

"Jake, I forgive you."

Jake doesn't take the bite he was about to take, but still looks straight ahead. In an irritated voice, he asks, "What?"

"I forgive you, Jake."

"Well... what does that mean?"

"I'm tryin' to figure that out. I know it doesn't mean that the anger an' disappointment an' shame will just go away, or that what you did just gets erased. That isn't gonna happen very easy. But it might mean that... that the love I have for you as your dad — yeah, that's what I said. I love you, Jake. I prob'ly haven't said that out loud often enough — the love I've had for you since the second you were born, that I had for you as you sat in that high chair over there, that I'll have for you 'til the day I die — that love comes first. Before the anger. Before the disappointment. Before the shame.

"I'm your dad. The only one you got. That puts me in kind of a special place. Forgivin' my own son... well, that should be a no-brainer. You should know that you can come to me an' not be afraid. That you can depend on me. Even when you've done somethin' wrong. You should know that you can come to me, an' that I'll work with you, not against you, no matter what."

He takes a bite of his cheeseburger as an awkward silence hangs between him and his son.

"I don't know that I've done such a good job so far. So just sayin' 'you can come to me' maybe won't mean much to you. I got work to do to make those words mean somethin'. We both got work to do. I can't do your work for you, Jake, but I can do mine."

He takes one more bite, then gives up on the cheeseburger.

"So for starters, you need to know that I forgive

you. For all you've done. To me. To this family. And to yourself. I don't know what it means yet, or how it works, but I forgive you, an' I mean it. I hope it can bring us both some peace."

Jake has still not looked at his dad. He still sits there, hunched over, looking at the wall. He's quiet, motionless, with his cheeseburger held over his plate with both hands. He can feel his dad looking at him. What does he want? Does he want me to say something? What am I supposed to say?

"So, what's the second thing?"

The dad hesitates. When he speaks, there is a catch in his throat. "Jake... I wanna ask you...

to forgive me."

The boy finally turns his head toward his dad, looking perturbed and puzzled. "What are you talking about?"

"You know that anger you feel toward me so often? That can't all be your fault. I need to accept my part of the blame for that. I'm your dad. But I don't think I've done the best job of that. I'm human. I've been pretty quick to anger myself. That's what I showed you, so that's what you learned. An' I learned it 'cause that's what my dad showed me. I'm afraid that if you have kids some day, they'll learn it, too. An' I'll hate knowin' that I was a part of that.

"So I'm askin' your forgiveness for everything

I've done wrong. An' for what I haven't done for you that I should've. For all I haven't given you. For the dad I haven't been.

"When you stand in front of that judge this afternoon, I'm gonna be standin' right next to you. Because when that judge judges you, he'll be judgin' me, too.

"We both got work to do, Jake. An' part of that work — maybe the hardest part — will be learnin' how to forgive each other. So, I'm givin' you my forgiveness, Jake. An' I'm askin' you to try to forgive me." He pauses. "You think you can?"

The boy looks down at his plate, silent and distant. Finally he mumbles, "I dunno."

The dad is left wondering if any of this has been worthwhile. Will it make any difference? Is this whole forgiveness thing just a waste of words? Does it mean anything to his son?

Then a small window of hope opens, as the boy speaks two more words.

"I'll try."

"That's all I ask."

Forgiveness. We should all be willing to ask for it, and we should all be willing to give it.
Because we all need it. Every one of us. Every day.
Including today.

LAUGHTER

In the middle of the cafe is a round table for six. There are eight men sitting around it, all with gray hair. Well, if they have any hair at all. On the table is a congregation of coffee mugs, several wrapped in big, weathered hands with thick, leathery fingers. They are hands that have been fixing, building, tilling and lifting for most of a lifetime.

These are the "reg'lars." And at the moment, seven of them are turned toward the eighth, listening to a story that has them all smiling and nodding, waiting for the punch line they've probably all heard before. "And so she says, 'Well, what did you expect at this time of night? Pancakes?'" The whole table explodes in laughter, old men with their heads thrown back, slapping their knees and shaking their heads in amusement.

"Well, he'll never ask her that ag'in!"

"Not if he ever wants to be let back inta the place, he won't."

As the laughter dies down to a murmur of chuckles, and coffee cups are lifted to grinning lips, the door jingles and all eight heads turn to see who's walking in.

"Harv!"

"Hey, Harv, good ta see ya!"

"Good ta be seen," answers the newcomer as he pulls an empty chair from over by the wall and slides into place in the space that opens up for him at the table. He looks toward the kitchen, catching Irene's eye and, with a quick lift of his chin, tells her all she needs to know. Within seconds one more steaming coffee cup joins the congregation.

"Nice t'have you back, Harv."

"Thanks, Irene. Not near as nice as it is to be back."

One of the men leans forward and asks slyly, "So, Harv, did them pretty nurses finally get their fill of ya and kick y'out?"

A ripple of ancient snickers rises, but all eyes are on Harv as he blushes and says, "Yeah, somethin' like that."

They would never admit it, but they had all been plenty concerned when Harv hadn't shown up for coffee a week ago. Irene, who always seems to know everything before anybody else does, had told them that he'd had an ambulance ride that morning. But they are plenty relieved to know that he is now out of that hospital and doing better. Their love for their friend, and for each other, is almost visible beneath the cover of their carefree chatter.

"When'd'ja get out?"

"Just this mornin'."

"This mornin'?! Wha'd'ja do, come straight here?"

"Yeah, I missed Irene's coffee."

Hoots of laughter fly toward the kitchen, and Irene throws a smiling dirty look right back.

"B'sides, I had to see if you boys been behavin' yerselves."

"Course not! D'ja think we'd change that much in a week?"

Wrinkled, weathered faces smile and bob

around the table.

"So, Harv," says the man who had told the pancake story, lowering his voice with genuine concern and leaning forward across the table, "did they git ya fixed up? Are ya feelin' okay now?"

"Yeah, I'm feelin' good. It's pretty amazin' what they can do these days. But I gotta tell ya, there was a while there when they didn't know if I was gonna make it."

Eight solemn faces nod knowingly. The pancake man looks down into the darkness of his coffee cup and says in a low and serious voice, "Well, Harv, I hate ta tell ya this..." He looks up from his coffee and into his friend's face, "but... well... ya didn't make it. And now ya gotta spend all of eternity... WITH US!" Howls of relieved laughter erupt and break the seriousness of the moment.

Another voice chimes in, "And, Harv, just so y'know, this ain't heaven." A flock of guffaws rises up from the table, circles in the slowly spinning blades of the ceiling fan, and gets spread out around the small cafe. The laughter is so loud and heartfelt that almost nobody notices when Harv, shaking his head, a big smile on his face, replies, "Well, it is to me."

Just then Irene arrives to pour more coffee. One of the men quips, "Yeah, have some more of Irene's coffee, Harv. That'll keep yer heart tickin'."

"Yeah, if it don't kill ya."

Chuckles of agreement get shuffled around the tableful of old friends. Irene, standing next to Harv with her plastic name tag at his eye level, says again, "Well, I'm mighty glad to see yer back, Harv."

And Harv, without missing a beat, looks at what's right in front of him and says, "Thanks, Irene. And I'm mighty glad to see yer front."

Irene's own voice is the loudest as whoops of laughter fill the room — the music of friendship, of gratitude, and, yes, of love. Harv is blushing a little at saying something so openly racy. But Irene, wagging her finger and shaking her head in mock disapproval, simply turns and retreats to her kitchen, smiling all the way.

Laughter. It's a cheerful medicine that can make anyone feel better. We should each have a dose of it every day.

PATIENCE

"This feels a little weird, Darren. It's been such a long time."

In the booth closest to the kitchen, next to where the juke box used to be, sits a young couple. He has eaten almost all of his open-face roast beef sandwich, and she has barely touched her grilled cheese.

"Don't you think it's just a little arrogant that you asked me to promise to wait for you, then you went away for... it seemed like forever."

"You knew I was away at college. But you

heard from me nearly every day." She raises an eyebrow, so he adds, "Well, I did say 'nearly'. And we've been together every time I came home."

"Oh, right. You fit me into your busy schedule when you had time. And in the meantime, you expected me to honor my promise and to just sit here, I don't know, knitting or something, waiting for you to return from your 'personal journey'."

She is quiet for a minute and pokes at her food.

"I did wait for you, Darren. I waited a long time. I got a job here at the clinic. I went to nursing school. I kept busy. But it felt like I was putting my own 'personal journey' on hold.

"Finally it felt like I was wasting my life, like I needed to meet some other guys, like I just didn't know what you were doing or whether you would ever come back for me. Or whether you even cared."

"Of course, I cared, Ruth. You were on my mind every day."

"Well, it sure didn't seem like it to me. So I started dating. And one of those relationships got pretty serious. I don't know if you even knew it, but he actually asked me to marry him."

"No, I didn't know. So... why didn't you?"

She is quiet for a while.

"Well... because... because it just seemed like I'd be marrying the wrong man. But... but where was the right man, Darren? What was he doing? He took off... for Italy!"

"You knew that after I got my degree in art, I needed to study in Florence."

"Right! You were in Florence, being the Renaissance Man, while I was supposed to stay here in this little tiny town, keeping the home fires burning and waiting for your glorious return."

Irene comes by to take their plates and doesn't say a word. But she and Darren give each other a secret look.

"Well, I have returned, Ruth. Just like I promised. I didn't realize it was going to take so long. I wanted to meet you here because of all the time we hung out here together in high school. This is where we had our first date. Remember?"

"Of course I remember. It was after that awful football game."

"I couldn't believe that you'd said yes when I asked you to come here with me. I was so dazzled by you, I just couldn't imagine that you'd want to be with me. I didn't think I was good enough for you."

"We spent a lot of time here together back then."

"We sure did. In this same booth. Right next to the juke box. There was a song that we both loved so much. We played it over and over, every time we were here. Do you remember it?"

"Of course I remember it. 'I'd Wait Forever' by the Foresters."

"That's why I wanted to meet you here today. In this same booth. I wanted to play that song for you again on the juke box. Just like we used to. But, well, I didn't realize that things had changed so much."

"That's right, Darren. Things have changed."

"I couldn't believe it when I walked in and the juke box was gone. So I guess I have no choice but to sing the song for you myself."

Darren had always had a pretty good singing voice. So, right there in Irene's Cafe, with the place nearly full during the lunch rush, Darren starts singing that old song to Ruth.

You know I'd wait forever,

Forever and a day.

What's a little waiting

If I can hear you say

That you will always love me

And promise to be true?

You know I'd wait forever

To spend forever with you.

Other customers in the cafe have turned to look. And when the song is over, there is a little flutter of applause. Darren is looking directly into Ruth's face, but Ruth is looking down at her hands, folded on the table in front of her, not knowing what to think or feel.

At that moment, Irene brings a plate with a piece of her famous Dream Cake and two forks. On top of the deep brown chocolate frosting sits a ring. A beautiful, unique gold ring with a single, perfect diamond set in a tiny shower of stars. She sets it on the table in front of a speechless Ruth and walks away with an uncontrollable smile on her face.

After a silent moment, Darren says, "I made it. For you."

Ruth looks at Darren with tears in her eyes. Tears of shock. Tears of love. Tears of confusion.

"From the time I went off to school and decided to major in art, I knew that I wanted to make something perfect for you. The best I could possible make. Because I knew how much I loved you. I started studying sculpture, then got interested in working with precious metals. But when I graduated, I knew I still wasn't good enough. So I went to Florence and apprenticed with a jewelry maker there, so I could learn the old, traditional ways. I wanted to make something as real and as perfect as I could make it.

"When I got back from Italy, I got a job working with a master goldsmith in Boston. He's made pieces for dignitaries and princes. Even presidents. He's getting old, and he's been waiting to find someone who could take over his studio, who could work in the old ways. He really likes my work, so last week he asked me if I would be willing to take over for him. It's a good job, Ruth. One that I will love, and that I can stay with for a long, long time."

He stops to let it all sink in.

"But I know that, even though I continue to do this for the rest of my life, and even though I may make jewelry for the most important people in the world, nothing will ever be as important to me as this ring. And no one will ever be as important to me as you. I love you.

"You've waited a long time, Ruth. But I'm going to ask you to wait just a little longer. I would like to meet you here next week, on Wednesday, in this same booth, at this same time. Then I'm going to ask you to marry me.

But I know that this is all very sudden, and very weird. So I want you to have time to think about it."

The entire cafe is completely silent. Tears are streaming down Ruth's face as she stares at that beautiful gold ring, nestled on top of that luscious piece of Dream Cake. Finally she looks up.

"Darren, I've waited for you for years. I'm tired of waiting. You used to be my best friend. I used to love you very much. During these years of waiting, I've realized that... that I will never have another friend like you, and I will never love anyone else like I love you. I won't make you wait, Darren. My answer... is yes."

They both blush as everyone in the cafe — the widow, the grandpa and the little girl, the teenager and his dad, all the reg'lars, the guy in the kitchen, Irene, and I — all burst into cheers and applause. As the noise settles down, the pancake man looks at Darren and says, "Well, what ya waitin' for? Kiss 'er!"

And he does.

Patience. It's worth working on, because some things are simply worth waiting for. And today could be the day.

GENEROSITY

I am just finishing the delicious banana cream pie that I shouldn't have ordered but couldn't resist, as Irene approaches my table.

"How's everything?"

"Everything was delicious, Irene. I'm so glad I found this place. It was just what I needed."

"I knew I'd never seen you in here before. Traveling?"

"Yes. Work. I don't usually stop at places like

this when I travel. I'm really glad I did."

"Yeah, this is what I call a 'slow food' joint. People only get served as quick as I can get around to 'em. But at least you know that here the food was cooked by a real human being."

"I see that. And I appreciate it. Sometimes it seems like real human beings are hard to find anymore."

"Naw. There are real people everywhere. Good people. You just have to be willing to see 'em."

"I suppose you're right. Thanks, Irene. I'll take

the check, please."

"No charge. It's on the house."

"Oh, no... no, I couldn't..."

"Oh, it's not just for you. It's for everybody. All day. Din'cha see the board?" She tosses her thumb over her shoulder toward the "Today's Special" chalkboard, where someone had written, "Yes it is."

"Well, yes, I saw it, but I didn't know what it meant."

"It means that today is a special day, so nobody

pays for anything. Not all day."

"But why?"

"I had a doctor appointment this morning. Had to open up late 'cause the hospital I have to go to is over 40 miles from here. At that appointment, I heard words that I didn't think I'd ever hear. The doctor told me that, for now, I'm 'cancer free'."

"You have cancer?"

"Did have. Breast. They caught it early, but still. Nobody wants to hear the 'c' word. So I told my doctor that I was ready to do whatever needed to be done. Even surgery. I was willing. But they can do miracles these days. They really can.

"Of course, it wasn't any fun. Some of those drugs made me feel pretty awful. And I lost all my hair. It's back now, but it used to be kinda straight, not all kinky like this.

"I was afraid I'd have to close up the cafe while I was goin' through the treatments. But the people around here — those good people that I told you are everywhere..." She looks around at the customers in her cafe. "Some of these people here — they wouldn't hear of it. Dave back there kept the kitchen goin', and these people came in on their own time to wait tables and wash dishes and whatever else needed to be done to keep the place open. They just gave and gave and gave."

She waves through the front window at someone passing by.

"So I told myself that if I ever heard those magic words, 'cancer free', I'd do something to pay these people back. I heard those words this morning. So today's pay day. Nobody who eats in Irene's Cafe today pays a single penny. Not even strangers." She looks me right in the eye and smiles. It isn't the smile of a stranger.

"So, y'see, today's special. But it's not special just because I say it is. Or just because I got good news this morning. Today's special just because it is. So was yesterday. And tomorrow will be, too. I know now how precious life is. How special every day should be. I don't ever want to forget."

As Irene turns and starts walking back toward the kitchen, I pull out several dollars to leave as a tip. An extra generous tip, of course. But she turns and sees me and just shakes her head, to let me know that, if I leave money on that table, it will probably still be there waiting for me when I come back.

And I will come back. I know that for sure.

I stand to leave, taking one more long look around Irene's Cafe and the customers there. I am leaving with a sense of satisfaction and well-being that I hadn't had when I walked in. It is only partly because of the food. As I reach to open the door, I hear Irene's voice holler from behind the counter, "Remember, today's special."

I turn, smile, and holler back, "Yes it is!"

Generosity. We can show it every day.

Not just in the way we give,

but in the gracious way we receive.

And a gift that we receive every day

is the certainty that Today's Special. Yes it is.

YES IT IS

It's been a hard week. And it's only Wednesday. But as I open the jingling door of Irene's Cafe and walk outside, I feel very different than when I went in. Now I have important work to do. I'd better not waste any more time.

And the first thing I need to do is make a phone call. I'm going to cut this trip short and go home. I need to make sure that what's good stays good. I need to pay attention to what's really important. I need to celebrate what I have before I go chasing after what I don't.

I need to enjoy the best that today has to offer, and not get distracted by all the other things on the menu.

That continental breakfast at last night's motel didn't amount to much. But what I got at Irene's Cafe is going to stay with me for a good long time.

Today's Special. Yes it is.